Nils Guttorp

HAIKUS

• from Fågeltofta •

Edited by Anna Guttorp

Translation and adaption by Peter Guttorp
and Elizabeth Dobromylskyj

© 2015 Anna Guttorp
Photos private if nothing else noted.

Printing and publishing: BoD

ISBN: 978-91-7463-580-5

Haiku is a kind of short poem, originating in Japan. It can be found in many variants. Nils is consistently following a strict form: every haiku has three lines. The first line contains five syllables, the second line has seven syllables, and the third line has five syllables.

Innehåll

Preface

Nils Guttorp
1920-2013

My father was an artist and a musician. He spent his first years in a country school in Sunnanå, but soon the family moved to Lund, and there he lived until he was over fifty years old, when he and his wife Inga moved to Österlen, the eastern part of the southernmost province of Sweden.

He devoted himself to painting during the forties and early fifties. In 1953 he got an organist's exam. He worked as kantor in Västerstad and Östraby until 1960, later in Kävlinge, and eventually in Vitaby and Södra Mellby.

In 1980 Inga and Nils moved to Fågeltofta school. In 2001 he was left behind there, but lived there until the summer of 2012.

He was very fond of the house in Fågeltofta, and these haiku poems were written there. He had started a book, but did not follow through. I, his daughter, have collected his papers and chosen the poems and pictures for this book.

Anna Guttorp 2013

Ambition

To posterity
I give as my testament
this book of haikus.

> Some lines are written
> only for my own reason.
> That does not suffice.

It is obvious:
Things that are easy to make
constitute no art.

> My inspiration
> has made the occasional
> text truer than truth.

A competition:
To place these different words
in the right order.

> Is there a new life
> also for my memories?
> No one inherits.

In this collection
is no particular rhyme.
Maybe some reason.

Is it possible
that your body remembers
the generations?

Lighting the night lamp
I am writing these words down
facing towards the wall.

Nils.
Photo: Ulf Giertz.

In Fågeltofta

The bureacracy
thinks that we are landowners.
But that is not so.

Made ventilation.
This domicile is breathing
better than myself.

The exercises:
shovel snow and mow the lawn
keep me in good shape.

Wall paper patterns
can be as uplifting as
organ works by Bach.

Inga and Nils.

In a white guest room
I let paint and gravity
make vertical stripes.

Want to paint pictures.
Conflict of priorities.
It will be windows.

Gardening amateur
in the true meaning am I.
It's invisible.

        I made a haiku,
        I was outside. It was good.
        Now I forgot it.

Five times I painted
the workshop ceiling in vain.
I had cataracts.

        Sometimes I can hear
        sounds I attribute to mice.
        It is my stomach.

From the phrase "plum grove"
we were inspired to plant
forty damson shoots.

        Under our maple
        leaves form an exemplary
        textile print pattern

In Fågeltofta

The voles and myself
are competing for the lawn.
The voles are winning.

                    Makes a nice pattern,
                    the neighbouring acacia
                    against our maple.

By the lily pond.
The frog is sitting on a stone.
Soon it makes Mah-Jong.

                    A branch, fallen down,
                    immediately settles
                    calmly as a cat.

There was snow last night.
Must shake the juniper bush.
It is too pretty.

                    It is not the cars,
                    it is only the snowplow
                    that one hears tonight.

Woodworking

A good local phrase:
"After autumn carpenter."
I am one of them.

It's desirable
to make a tactile sculpture
which can be worn out.

Start with the subject.
When you determined the form
it has been altered.

I carved me a fox.
But quite soon it was stolen.
Favourable critique.

Vignette to Lunds folkskolors historia. Linocut by NG.

Woodworking

Under the clutter
there may be something splendid.
Bring out a notion!

                    My material
                    must exhibit resistance
                    to keep together.

Accurate drilling
is needed so that a screw
easily goes in.

                    I searched and I found.
                    Was looking for some papers
                    but found a hole punch.

Why is it that a
seed dispenser must look like
a gingerbread house?

                    Paint store catalogues
                    give us a small sample of
                    possibilities.

Haiku patterns

The haiku's form fence
(you may not climb over it):
five, seven and five.

> The haiku content
> may partly be affected
> by the length of words.

Sustainable forms
like sonnet and limerick
helped me get started.

> Even in short poems
> all can be formulated
> except for "Nothing."

Give me a subject
Then I will take away words
to make poetry.

> Why I like haiku?
> Japanese daughter-in-law
> is partly to blame.

First and second person

Grammatically
I'm first person singular
and you are second.

Bereft of content
one cannot write poetry.
Although I do that.

If I lack hindrance
– in hospital or prison –
I promise to come.

I hurry slowly.
I may often promenade
but scurry, never.

Engaged.

Here are my deep roots:
in art, the impressionism
in the music, jazz.

Despite a whole lot
of things that happened to me,
you are the best one.

Sitting in my thoughts.
Therefore I always get scared
by the telephone.

Although my height is
only five feet five inches
it's far to the ground

I'm calm as a cat.
But just like the cats, I am
easily frightened.

The difficulties
challenge me to a duel,
and I will take part.

Don't exaggerate.
If you want all to follow,
you'll be losing me.

How many are we?
Sometimes we are only two.
Other times billions.

Second person

The one you once saw
you will never see again.
All changes, as you do.

A greenhouse effect:
don't cultivate your feelings.
Then they become false

Inga.

Adapt yourself first
to the usual straitjacket.
Later you may change.

A stretched dialogue:
a few words every half hour
can yield good contact.

Honorable you.
let me now get to know you.
You're amiable.

Once you have mastered
three hundred regulations
there will be new ones.

Seeking and finding,
begging, getting response. But
may I ring the bell?

Important to know,
bad personal chemistry
can be amended.

It is evident
that what has been done is done.
Yet: please forgive me!

I think I know it, how your
dream becomes the truth.
There, I said it now.

Sometimes I need you
to keep your fingers crossed. Then
I am most grateful.

I was raking leaves.
Then the memory struck me:
Maple syrup scent!

To write poetry

Sometimes it's easy,
sometimes it takes many weeks
to find the right words.

> The usual phrases
> I would like to utilize
> in a new fashion.

Verse is more than lies
also more than verity.
Verse is reality.

> No more parables!
> Poetry of realism
> suffices for me.

Although natural,
words and music should arrive
quite surprisingly.

> When writing verses
> the content by itself is
> only a pretext.

It comes of itself.
If you compel poetry
your stomach will hurt.

> My dearest reader!
> If you relish a poem
> do learn it by heart.

A recitation
must be wholly literal.
Deviations: none

> Such a character
> that it sticks in memory
> should a poem have.

Vignette to Lunds folkskolors historia. Linocut by NG.

To write poetry

Words are like timber.
Much ends up on the ground as
the topic takes shape.

> As to poetry
> I would like to imitate
> the composer Haydn.

I have requested
from Jakob Book-seller
poems in Finnish.

> Light and elegant
> must be the appearance of
> the poem. That's hard.

If I change my style:
Some taste for the absurd will
likely be maintained.

> This I don't want: To
> write a poem that ends with
> the words "Such is life."

Authors

Genius Goethe
his great colour theory
was grand poetry.

The simple word "Love."
I agree with Lars Forsell:
it is so much more.

When Benvenuto
writes "My dear reader," then I
take the compliment.

He said: Our Selma
likes women. What about it?
I do that as well.

Light-enthusiasm
(a sweet word by Ekelöf)
I do wish us all.

Anders Österling
wrote about Ale's stones, but
saw not the colors.

Authors

Hasse and Tage
had a Schubertian sense
for recitation.

The twilight landscape
that Lagerkvist writes about
it is mine, Skåne.

Think of Piraten.
There are higher truths than those
that really happened.

Just like Nils Ferlin
I ask God to forgive me
some of my stanzas.

Behold the lilies
urges Evert Taube in his
waltz from Sjösala.

As Oscar Wilde once said,
the worst thing about old age
is that you're still young.

Quibbling

Thou shalt not quibble
is another commandment.
I do not keep it.

For you to speak up
is almost the same thing as
for you to speak out.

Too commonly used:
the expression "As it were"
in speech, so to speak.

When someone tells me:
You belong to one of them
I answer: which one?

Sometimes you need to
hold your tongue, or maybe put
your hand to your mouth.

Duck family. Linoprint by NG.

Childhood

Mother always made
the rolls different sizes.
It suited us well.

No malevolence.
An organ grinder is what
I wanted to be.

The siblings: Ruth, Ingrid, Gunnel, Nils.

I was mischievous
and some say that I still am.
But this, too, shall ass.

Say, what will you be
when you grow up? they ask me.
I'll never do that.

Boiled pike for dinner.
Butter, grated horseradish
necessary too.

We got angel cake
sometimes with "non" put in front.
It tasted better.

My grandfather was
an organist, said to have
adopted baroque.

Sold his village shop,
did not want to cheat people.
Became church warden.

I sat opposite
when Ruth was learning to read.
Guess the consequence!

When young, my mother
talked quietly with horses.
Got quiet answers.

Our ancestors who
went before us perhaps are
watching over us.

When young

Of course we were poor,
but we did not notice it.
Such luxuriance!

I was never cold
when painting in winter chill.
Until afterwards.

Mother and child. Pastel by NG.

My beloved wife
shares most of my interests.
Solidarity.

The interiors
were my favourite subjects
often with a view.

An artist comrade
treated us to bouillabaisse
a long time ago.

Independent? Sure!
Art school taught me to use oil.
But I showed gouache.

Art

The naturalism
is old-fashioned in painting,
novel in music.

> The evidence of
> the artist's loneliness is
> all of his paintings.

To make a copy
if you don´t want to improve
is superfluous.

> The question of why
> will only be answered by
> the final artwork.

These installations.
Some think that they are modern.
But it is not so!

> Pictures, parables.
> Perspective view shortening
> yields depth dimension.

Konst

Stenbocksgatan. Gouache by NG.

At Stenbocksgatan
I have often painted roofs.
No, paintings of roofs.

> All of the details
> must be of significance
> for the whole picture.

Computer, white wall.
A short-sleeved shirt. A man of
discretionary hues.

Painters

Self-confident man,
Leonardo da Vinci.
His writing mirrored.

Helene Schjerfbeck,
Paula Modersohn-Becker
and Käthe Kollwitz!

Vermeer was born then:
sixteen hundred thirty-two.
All Swedes know that year.

The art of Rembrandt!
I hardly think anyone
knows how he did it.

A drawing by Skum
looks like the Vasalopp-start
taken from above.

Try to discover
the motive in a landscape
by Gunnar Norrman.

Painting

Go from black to white
over yellow, green, blue, red.
It is possible.

> Don't ask me about
> which color I like the best,
> all is relative.

Christian esthetics:
If your right hand gets too good
paint with the left one!

> This is how it is:
> Mix many happy colours
> to get a grey tinge.

The color values
lie very close together
in the light of dusk.

> Good watercolors
> are all improvisations
> with plenty of luck.

Trivial objects
are studied in a still-life.
There's beauty in that.

The blazer. Pastel by NG.

A painter's knowledge:
It is the light surfaces
that are expansive.

The composition,
not the subject of the art,
is the real motive.

What I'll be painting
I see on the cornea
when my eyes are closed.

Horizontal line
positioned at eye level
is good for the soul.

Exhibiting

"This is what I've seen.
Please try to look the same way."
says the piece of art.

It will be no art
unless you hold your public
in highest esteem.

The picture frame must
not be very expensive.
Nor must the picture.

The artistic skill
must have an undertaking.
Please teach us something!

View with a mirror.
Classical Chinese paintings
are read from the right.

I like to get praise.
Impertinent flattery
I can't tolerate.

From the exhebition 1948.

Pedagogy

Am of teachers' stock.
Pedagogical burden
is leaving its mark.

We know too little.
I want both to educate
and, not least, to learn.

You have been gifted
by Nature herself with your
curiosity.

Don't think about style
try to work efficiently
then it will succeed.

The problems belong.
They are an essential part
of the solution.

What you do not know
always seems impossible
until you learn it.

Pedagogy

Don't be prejudiced!
Touch and musicality
Can all be practiced.

> Every last exam
> is a manifestation
> of lack of knowledge.

You are talented.
Don't believe that it's too hard,
I trust in you.

> Freedom by itself
> does not help anybody
> to choose direction.

There are people who
try to improve on themselves.
We thank them therefore.

> Worthy of study
> are manifold entities
> and humanity.

You do not want to
repeat a failure. Therefore
it is a good thing.

> Your self-confidence
> should not be too excessive
> but legitimate.

Don't want to show off,
but I do fall in that trap.
I'm sure you've noticed.

Tulips

A bunch of tulips
with three colours in the leaves,
two in the flowers!

The sound arising
from friction of tulip leaves
against each other.

Inside a tulip,
white, lit from the side, the tone
indescribable.

Too costly, you thought.
I'm going to buy tulips.
This we have need for.

Tulips. Fabric print by NG.

Nature

Studying nature
can be done in many ways.
Mine is the painter's.

Having a green thumb?
A dirty index finger
is good for flowers.

Non-artificial
"maculate" conception: it
is a miracle.

Nature is painting
in all the old-fashioned styles
and the coming ones.

The material,
the nature experience,
the composition.

At Sandhammaren
you see from the horizon
that the Earth is round.

Nature

Like Mount of Olives
Stenshuvud can be preaching:
No more disquiet!

People, tones, colours –
all get their significance
from the surroundings.

There was snow last night.
Not much paint is required
for watercolours.

The dairy in Lund.
Watercolor by NG.

Music

Music does describe
what cannot be reported
by other means.

The jazz is often
both for listener and player
quite captivating.

In a melody
with natural tone of voice
one believes the text.

Improvisation
must originate within
so as to reach out.

The twelve bar blues can
actually be applied
to psalmodic hymns.

This is how to sound
even in classical music:
Extemporaneous.

Music

All these drinking songs:
Not so many of them have
their own melody.

Sound in nature films
not always so credible:
Orchestral music.

Some of our chorales
must have been in existence
well before composed.

The baroque music:
mischievous in the repeats.
Belongs to the style.

Role in folk music
for the second violin:
listen, smile, respond.

In a jam-session
my feet are always playing
yet another voice.

Music producer
is not the one reading notes
but the one writing.

Useful for the soul:
preceding the closing beat
pause with fermata.

Johann Sebastian Bach. Das Wohltemperierte Klavier, Title page.

Musicians

There are hash slingers
just as generous as is
Ella Fitzgerald.

> The love of mankind
> is the origin of jazz.
> Think of Ellington!

After Basie's death
there really is no one left
to build pianos.

> Beethoven in his
> fourth piano concerto
> is splendidly drunk.

Although so simple
Basie's touch was exactly
inimitable.

> This is a power:
> so many more composers
> have done the same thing.

"Much too many notes"
the Emperor told Mozart.
Right, to the wrong man.

Quiet, what is this?
Johan the Evangelist
(Sebastian Bach).

Did you hear Astaire?
Some great percussion solos
right there on the floor.

Learn from Heinrich Schütz.
He knows why he is singing.
This, then, is voice care.

Polite child, Tatum,
who from his wild excursions
comes back home in time.

Meeting with colleagues,
discussing our church music,
vital in my trade.

Musicians

But Armstrong surely
was more than screaming metal.
He was blessed with love.

I was included!
"Good evening, everybody"
said Louis Armstrong.

He loved everyone.
His voice was instrumental.
The instrument sang.

Between speech and song
generous human being
with silver trumpet.

A break by Armstrong
which only was an onset
left us all sweating.

Louis Armstrong.

Practice

When I'm practicing
I want to be all alone
in my cubicle.

If you practice wrong
your fingers learn the errors.
They are coming back!

Despite readiness,
brought about through practicing,
no one is ready.

How does it sound to
listen to a breaking string?
Unexceptional.

You must at least hope
that superior playing will
raise the audience.

Each of the repeats
may just as well be varied
for the sake of change.

Performance

Play printed music.
It is just reproducing.
Do it anyway.

You see furrowed brows
on the violin players.
Sends the wrong message.

A light, warm applause
while the music still goes on:
successful solo.

Keep the tempo down.
Beware of pomposity
in the fast movements.

Here is some advice:
look happy while you're singing.
That makes you sound good.

Let the people hear
that your classical music
is new for today.

Music is a feast.
I demand the right to laugh
during the concert.

It can go too fast.
You need to have time to feel
in an allegro.

Interpretation
is to show your point of view
to the composer.

You have to listen
not just sit there quietly
during the music.

Dogs as well as kids
ogle like curling players
at my tap dancing.

Take some liberties
when playing the cembalo.
Perhaps it will show.

Birds

We are feeding birds.
The little birds get their seeds.
The hawk: little birds.

Pay close attention
to the song of the blackbird.
He's a musician.

A snowless winter.
We need the feathered creatures.
They do not need us.

In early morning
the robin is playing its
minipiccola.

Was it a chaffinch?
Maybe a willow warbler?
Icterine warbler!

For twenty years straight
we celebrated sunrise
with Dagny-breakfast.

Song

The egregious
which cannot be put in words
should perhaps be sung.

Don't require faith
from a church choir singer
but note faithfulness.

Rules should be followed.
Improvised choir singing
cannot manage that.

A two-part canon;
could well be a simple song,
although it's double.

Sense of unity
present in unison song,
heightened in canon.

Collective slogans
texts of praise and of malign
are good for canons.

Counterpoint

The counterpoint school
requires cooperation
more than possible.

> I know all the laws
> and when it's necessary
> I opt out of one.

Many solutions
are to be selected from
in the counterpoint.

> It may be this way:
> counterpoint education
> helps me with writing.

On the final tone:
a plagal cadence coda
made out of eight chords.

> A people's culture
> which manages polyrhythm
> is in Africa.

Time passes

All the things one learns
will probably be of use
at some other time.

How I know, and where,
but don't ask about when; weak
short term memory.

Nils in the garden.

The twenty hundreds.
But the third millenium
is too large for us.

Follow summer time
but am not changing the clock.
Reality check.

The watch batteries
never last for quite as long
when time goes by fast.

Cast down with an oath
the wristwatch started ticking.
Works of the devil!

Metaphysics

Confession of faith:
I find it hard to doubt that
God believes in me.

Try to understand.
Realize the uselessness.
It is arrogant.

Our prerequisites:
To discover is divine.
To seek is human.

From time to time come
the improbabilities
which are a greeting.

It is sought by all
although under different
names: help, truth, Allah ...

Expecting visit.
Come now, oh Holy Spirit
and let's get to work.

Saul and David. Screen print by NG

At some other place
there is a focus of truth
outside time and space.

The concentration
is a mobilization
of higher forces.

All that will happen
is as much reality
as that which has been.

What is religion?
An event of reasoning
going up and down.

Religion teaches
that there is indeed a truth
and that life exists.

The monotheists
all believe in the same god
or is it not so?

Metaphysics

In case I were God
I would not permit people
to prove that I was.

Keeping fingers crossed
is just a variant of
the clasping of hands.

On God's existence,
which is indisputable,
there is much debate.

Believing in God?
Many think that truth exists.
But God is the truth.

To forgive someone
is to be forgiven too.
This is happiness.

Since God is the truth,
the atheist is very
sophisticated.

Faith and science

In telepathy
science begins to believe.
I have evidence.

Like many others:
The existentialism
is also a faith.

There's no randomness
once you view it carefully.
But it has humour.

Have you faith in God?
the journalist queried Per.
"If he has in me."

To question all that
which has not yet been proven
I call prejudice.

The first Christians
restricted their communism
to the believers.

Faith and science

There is no symbol
in the mathematics world
that means everything.

A fine equation.
Speech is turned to poetry
by one´s fantasy.

Odd numbers are like
the inchworm at the border.
Stretches over it.

Is there randomness?
I know a statistician
who thinks it's doubtful.

The atheist's faith.
He has pursued and found you:
the great Nobody.

You believe in life?
Your atheism is a sham
you old rascal you.

Computers

Human encryption
computers can interpret.
Not animal speak.

New millenium
is not really an event
but for computers.

It is not often
computers show human traits,
like making mistakes.

People can do more.
The computer can only
do things possible.

Do computers joke?
They hyphenate manslaughter
between s and l.

On the back pages
of the computer printouts
I write, just by hand.

Other places

In an unknown place
I´d like to get lost, of course
but just lost enough.

> A dead-end street is
> the Path of Virtue, Norrtälje.
> The same is true here.

The Briton disclaims
while the Yankee does welcome
when you say "Thank you."

> Only woods and hill.
> I find myself so confined
> with no horizon.

The road signs tell me
what speed I am travelling
on little byways.

> Regardless of which
> of many possible routes
> I travel forward.

Without overview
all roads are going straight on
until the next curve.

California
has "Sentimental journey"
in its melody.

The jokk from afar
sounds almost like the ore train
from even farther.

After mountain hikes
one can sit for quite a while
and just remember.

The mountain nature
through its texture and colour
makes humans artists.

Stockholm is pretty.
But nowadays I find it
overly distant.

Sports

For improved vision
I brought my spectacles case
to the arena.

One must keep fighting,
we are taught by the athletes.
But the targets change.

My favourite sport:
Free dressage ride with music,
horse thought controlled.

Sport regulations
can be improved as needed.
Public interest.

The nationalism
must be limited to just
the sports arenas.

The path is winding
but the competitors want
to go very straight.

Quite close to the frame
stands the trusted goalkeeper.
That's why he's lucky.

An assessment sport
could football possibly be
but the goals still count.

Hazard element
contributes to the football's
popularity.

Football is culture
Hooliganism no culture.
What is occultism?

It's a puzzlement:
Sometimes I am medial
regarding football.

It sounds curious:
There is in veteran sports
an influx of youth.

Sports

8.95

Time and space records:
long jump, one hundred meters
are getting closer.

*The world record in long
jump is getting …-*

Put in "one hundred,"
More effort you can't put in
whatever you say.

All competitors
in both pole vault and high jump
miss the last attempt.

No experience
does give you a handicap
similar to golf.

It amuses them
to play for their home country
who're living abroad.

Grey at a distance
appears the Vasalopp crowd
although colorful.

9.58

The sport biathlon
has military background
which we may forget.

Struggle in TV
between the production team
and the ski trade marks.

The alpine skiers
travel down an average
between blue and red.

The ski jump event
really should take longer time
than jumps in downhill.

It's fascinating
how much of psychology
there is in hockey.

Who is there to blame?
The ice hockey team, or you
who did not watch them?

Politics and money

A basic error:
You are voting with your feet
Go to the meetings!

> The true socialism
> we will probably not see
> until in heaven.

The historians
think that there has always been
religious conflicts.

> All political
> parties seem to want the same
> but never agree.

The politicians.
Comparing to what they know
they're too powerful.

> If our history
> leads us to nationalism
> we should forget it.

Questions of feeling
are not very suitable
for referendum.

They are publishing
the medical novelties
earlier than good.

All human beings
are worthy of food, lodging,
clothes, entertainment.

How many weapons?
How many can they murder?
How many are there?

Mahogany things:
Even if they are for free
they are too costly.

We are responsible:
Preventing catastrophes
may be our duty.

Politics and money

Respect your neighbour,
consider all your colleagues.
Join the union!

Sjöbo election.
That I do not have blue eyes
gives me some pleasure.

No politicians!
Let competence be in charge
at our hospitals.

The good journalists
are supposed to ask stupid
questions in their work.

Even there below
the salaries of workers:
Another abyss.

Do accountancy
I am incapable of.
Will not get to it.

Without property
you only receive respect
from your companions.

Today's poverty:
Can only use five-hundreds
at the gas station.

Double taxation
is paying your income tax
with value added.

I doubt both of them:
whether market economy
is democracy.

View from the school in Fågeltofta.

Gastronomy

Perhaps the sharpest
cheese I never got to taste
I saw in New York.

> The white mold cheeses
> sometimes are at a bargain.
> That's when they are best.

Peel of an orange
can often be very dry
and the fruit juicy.

> Do you enjoy food?
> Then you must admit freely
> that nature aids you.

Even in Konsum:
ninety-nine cents too many
for all things they sell.

> You need recipe,
> some leaning over backwards,
> a teaspoon of luck.

Positive items
such as parsley, dill and thyme
I will write about.

                    Taste wants aroma
                    as well as consistency.
                    Also appearance.

How about this one:
Ginger bread, butter and cheese,
on top marmalade.

                    Bodily reasons
                    dictate fasting more than the
                    spiritual ones.

Sear and boil in milk
split mackerel. Bone left in.
Chopped chives over it.

                    A well cured priest cheese
                    can even the organists
                    serve to each other.

Gastronomy

Many vegetables,
broth weak, boil suitably long.
Sune's own fish soup.

> To spit out the wine
> av wine testers are wont to
> I shall never learn.

Even bananas
whose outside is fully black
can be of first class.

> Setting a table
> requires the addition
> of convincing things.

I will try to sow
the bread spice cardamom in
the vegetable patch.

> A ripened apple
> must be kept in your pocket
> until forgotten.

Church and organ

In the church it is
not always the homily
which is paramount.

Regardless of sound
an imitation of organ
is sacrilegious.

Never talk about
alcohol-free communion
wine. It is just juice.

Alone in the church.
Two-way communication
from the organ bench.

Colouristical
and not in the least white-washed
is our church's arch.

A surprising tune
Easter Introitus does
describe the wonder.

Church and organ

Song of praise in church.
When the rhetoric is done
the music will speak.

> Gregorian chant:
> a mystical dimension
> which may well function.

It is the sinners
who attend the church service
and nobody else.

> The lithurgical,
> which many are ignoring,
> important to me.

The vicar should know
that there are people listening
to postludia.

> The right church music
> is not art for the people
> but spiritual.

Every church organ
should sometime during its life
reach artistic peak.

Some of the chorals
must have existed before
they were written down.

Organ construction:
A fantastic profession
that lives in my dreams.

Let me now master
an organ disposition
with fifteen voices.

This is in earnest:
I want to build an organ
but don't have the time.

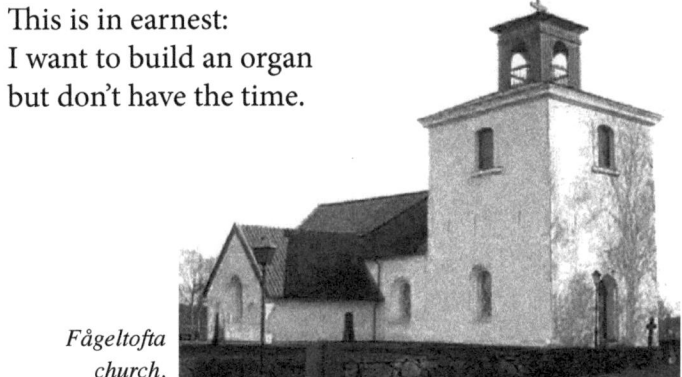

*Fågeltofta
church.*

Fun and games

Solve crosswords with ink.
That teaches you to reflect
(and how to retouch).

> Look at the children:
> How seriously they play,
> how much fun they have.

Laying art puzzle.
Do not look at the picture
until it's finished.

> Play a solitaire.
> By natural exaction
> it will not work out.

There are rules for all,
although some of them have not
yet been discovered.

> A plain deck of cards
> possesses many secrets
> which only God knows.

Reading and crosswords.
Leisure activities, not
wasting your spare time.

Pegas. Linoprint by NG.

The moments of joy
are needed in athletics
as well as in art.

Do you play tennis?
Win the appropriate balls
and you win it all!

Big competition.
All win a first place award.
I want to do that.

The dice were saying:
Bother probabilities!
In the end I won.

Seasons

Winter-spring landscape
White, ochre also grey, black,
a lithography.

Oh, the green winter!
May it last until Easter.
Then the spring snow comes.

Imperceptibly,
as when a swing turns over,
ends the vernal day.

I'm fantasizing:
What if the summer would come
here to us this year?

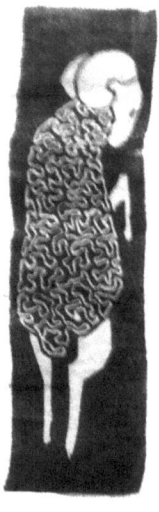

Spring is prosaic.
The poetic nightingale
is not dwelling here.

Spring apple blossoms
are better than their image
which is very good.

Program for finches
now that the time has arrived:
pair aerobatics.

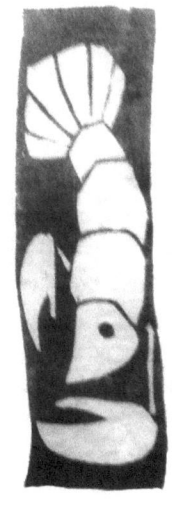

When it is summer
both day and night are coming
later than before.

At this time of year
winter season is starting.
Can we manage it?

The sun is shining.
The dandelions tell us
where they are living.

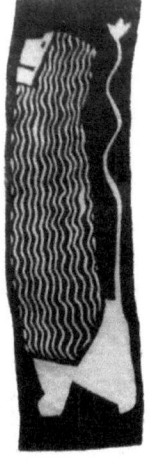

My recollection
of this very hot summer
is all that I drank.

The zodiak. Linoprint by NG.

Seasons

Thought about autumn:
We have learned how to require
changes of seasons.

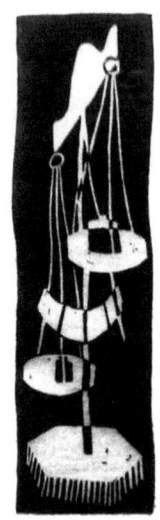

The light at this time
is certainly limited
but I consume it.

The trees outside here
experiment with rhythm
just like this haiku.

All Saints Day colours.
Between light black and dark white
appears the landscape.

Don't light the candle!
See how the colour blossoms.
Let it go to seed.

Expecting daylight,
both the winter night and I.
It usually comes.

Now in winter time
I will manufacture toys
for my grandchildren.

All the snow patches
enhance the other colours
as does a white shirt.

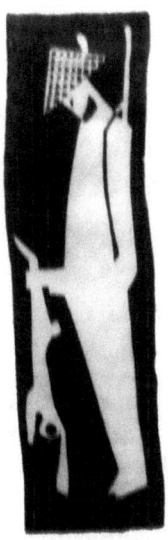

Snow landscape in sun
should have a function akin
to light therapy.

Snow in the furrows
ice-covered inundation
and tan rye stubble.

The weather

When weather is nice
the shadows are reflecting
the colour of the sky.

The weather forecast
is certainly coming true
sooner or later.

Affecting weather
some want to be able to.
But that will cause war!

When it's been raining
herbs and fragrances arise.
Colouring deepens.

Flash of genius
goes between heaven and earth
like flash of lightning.

The archbishop does
not believe very much in
weather predictions.

The lights and the smells
are right now my salute words:
Good morning, Sergeant!

> This greyish weather
> is containing very much
> notably colour.

Powers of nature,
like those of humanity,
supernatural.

> These patches of snow:
> Would like to be able to
> see them from above.

A good friend and I
liked to talk about weather.
We don't any more.

When Mother was ill ───

She rarely tired
in her professional life.
It is long ago.

> Now that you are ill,
> that I need to support you
> is a help for me.

You took off your shoes.
They are facing each other.
Makes me feel good.

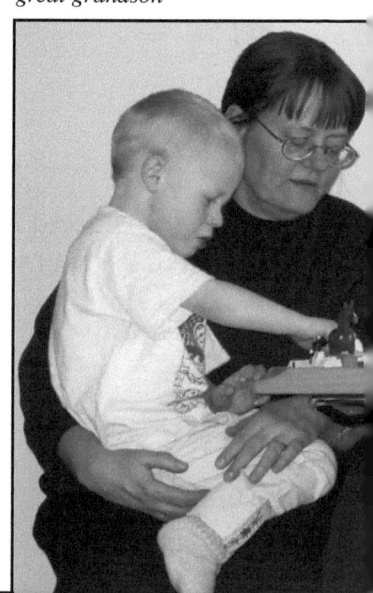

*Inga with daughter and
great grandson*

Why am I so glad
when you are being depressed?
Because you are here.

You have lost all your
initiative about chores.
That must be painful.

You do not have strength
and therefore you become sad.
Not what doctor thinks.

We are experienced,
so nowadays we rather watch
kid's shows on TV.

> Look around yourself,
> don't worry about a thing.
> It will all work out.

He understood so well,
the doctor reassured us.
But it was not true.

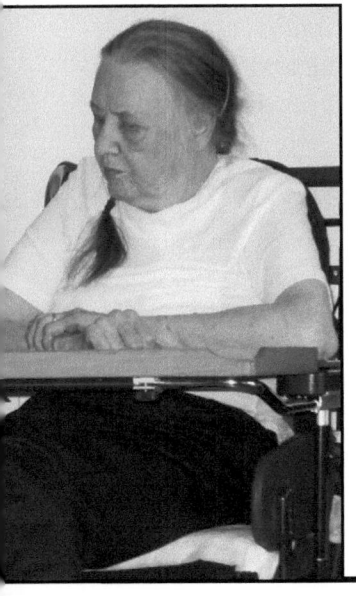

> It was so awful
> that you refused to receive
> children, grandchildren.

> I am so grateful.
> You forgave me so I could
> exculpate my fiend.

> This I've been saying
> after more than fifty years.
> Now you are secure.

Own health

My latest dress shirt
does not agree with my shape.
I am positive.

I dropped a quarter.
I see it on the carpet.
But it's too far down.

Hand gets to wash hand.
In my case it's also so:
foot gets to wash foot.

Here's a rarity:
I am working and resting
more than I need to.

My body tells me
when I'm too effervescent
or I sleep too much.

Without any thought
most of us can be breathing
in the open air.

Every night trouble:
My dreams tend to go slower
just as my breathing.

> To pass a border
> is more or less difficult,
> like falling asleep.

Not from disquiet.
My duodenal ulcer
I get from pleasure.

> A landscape I saw
> made me lay awake all night
> only from pleasure.

Fighting in the sleep.
When the blood stops running cold
then I am awake.

> Difficult breathing.
> The winter night continues.
> I will not do that.

Medicine

My heart and my lungs
encounter difficulties:
my doctor can't hear.

We do not want this.
If you ask a surgeon, he
wants to operate.

It's to no avail
to believe that happy pills
can help someone sick.

Examination
cost absolutely nothing.
Parking, however.

Since our physicians
do not believe our statements
we also doubt their.

Hospital emblem. Linoprint by NG.

Age

My associates
from school and military
are so few and old.

> There is much to do.
> My small pension is enough
> but the time is not.

I must say something
about old friends and friendships.
This will be enough.

> About us retirees:
> A long enough vacation
> we will never get.

The segregation
into age categories
does not improve things.

> A sign of the times:
> Having white and even teeth
> indicates old age.

Age

Take me as I am.
My zoot suit does not look good
without my long hair.

Age should be counted
(although that's impossible)
from the other side.

Seventy – eighty
years with toil and trouble are
invaluable.

The times are changing
faster than humanity.
Lower pension age!

To be retired
includes a certain amount
of loss of prestige.

Always and never –
in point of fact the same length –
as a turn of phrase.

*Ruth and Nils
with their father.*

Seize the day! I know
a blind one whose hobby is
to take photographs.

The language changes.
We need to understand this
little by little.

A horse can walk on,
can trot evenly and swift.
Burst forth in gallop!

Give me some more time!
I want opportunity
to charge batteries.

Learn new languages,
possible recreation
in my future life.

Have a lot to do.
High level of urgency.
Doubtful time access.

The Last Things

One thing is certain.
Personal experience
of it has no one.

A hopeless third death.
Whether to heaven or hell
we must separate.

Friends and relatives
who went before on purpose
I can't understand.

Obtaining knowledge
is not very attractive
as far as I know.

Can words be possessed?
"Never more" are sorrowful.
The word "soon" is mine.

I've long been seeking.
Now I'm able to say that
but I do not dare.

Final

My dearest reader!
I hereby do inform you
that I'm fond of you.

What I have written
– nothing to do about it –
is a self-portrait.

Please remember me,
not like I sometimes behaved,
but with joyousness.

Wanted to avoid
using the expression "life."
failed to do so.

True art addresses
all of the human beings
and at every time.

Self-portrait.
Linocut by NG

Thanks to my friends for the help!
Thanks to Jakob for the support!
Thanks to Father for the assignment!

Anna